C000179635

THE LAST DAYS OF STEAM IN
CAMBRIDGESHIRE

THE LAST DAYS OF STEAM IN
CAMBRIDGESHIRE

-ERIC SAWFORD-

ALAN SUTTON

First published in the United Kingdom in 1991 by
Alan Sutton Publishing Ltd · Phoenix Mill · Stroud · Gloucestershire

First published in the United States of America in 1991 by
Alan Sutton Publishing Inc. · Wolfeboro Falls · NH 03896–0848

Copyright © Eric Sawford 1990

All rights reserved. No part of this publication may be
reproduced, stored in a retrieval system, or transmitted,
in any form or by any means, electronic, mechanical photocopying,
recording or otherwise, without the prior permission of the
publishers and copyright holder.

British Library Cataloguing in Publication Data

Sawford, E.H. (Eric H.)
    The last days of steam in Cambridgeshire.
    1. East Anglia. Steam locomotives, history
    I. Title
    625. 26109426

    ISBN 0-86299-787-9

Library of Congress Cataloging in Publication Data applied for

Typeset in 9/10 Palatino.
Typesetting and origination by
Alan Sutton Publishing Limited.
Printed by Bath Press Ltd., Avon

Introduction

Cambridgeshire in the last years of steam provided much interest, ranging from the immaculate 'Top Link' A4s of the King's Cross and Haymarket depots, working the non-stop 'Elizabethan', to, at the other end of the scale, Cambridge, with its Great Eastern veteran E4 2–4–0 tender locomotives – still going strong on passenger duties during the fifties after a great many years in service.

The East Coast Main Line was the county's star attraction with its named 'Pacifics', the main line running north–south through the county from just north of Peterborough to a short distance south of St Neots, giving stretches of track where high speeds were permitted. After leaving Peterborough, where there were at one time severe speed restrictions through the station, today's line crosses the River Nene, passes various brickyards, now considerably decimated, and encounters the Fens at Holme and Connington before climbing to Abbots Ripton, once the site of a long-gone country station, before a run down the gradient to Huntingdon. After the station the line crosses the River Ouse and reaches Offord, the famous curves now no longer necessitating a severe speed restriction. Offord also had a station, though now, as with so many, no trace of it remains. After St Neots the line enters the neighbouring county of Bedfordshire. Several stations existed on the main line at one stage; as well as those mentioned there were Holme, Yaxley and Farcet. Now just three remain on the East Coast Main Line inside the county boundary: Peterborough, Huntingdon and St Neots.

Peterborough is still the most important railway centre within the county, with, besides the main line, routes to East Anglia, the Midlands and Lincolnshire. Several other routes existed in the fifties, the lines to Northampton, to Rugby and the M&GN line to the north Norfolk coast all bringing traffic to the city. There were large marshalling and shunting yards to deal with the considerable brick, mineral and general goods traffic, which are now just shadows of their former selves.

The major Peterborough locomotive depot was New England. This carried the shed code of 35A, though this was changed to 34E in the depot's last years. In 1950 the depot's allocation was 203 locomotives, in a wide variety of types and wheel arrangements. Another Peterborough depot existed, of a round-house design, which was originally operated by the London Midland Region, under the Nottingham district, but transferred to the Eastern Region on 13 August 1950 and became 35C, replacing its LMR shedcode of 16B. The depot then became known as Peterborough (Spital Bridge) with an allocation at that time of forty locomotives. By 1954 this had slightly increased as the total was forty-six, with a large number of Eastern Region classes replacing most of the previous allocation.

Locomotives on Spital Bridge allocation in 1954 were a mixed bag, with the LMR designs being represented by one solitary Ivatt 4MT and thirteen 4F 0–6–0s, the rest of the allocation consisting of Eastern Region types and four of the WD 2–8–0s, which were familiar in many parts of the country. Several veterans were also at the depot, including three of the Great Northern C12 4–4–2 tanks. A considerable number of this class were in the Peterborough area at this time; their duties included branch lines, carriage pilot and banking duties at Peterborough North. The sight and sound of these veterans as they banked heavy northbound passenger trains out of the station will long be remembered by those who can recall those days. Often the engine would slip if the rails were wet or greasy as it rounded the sharply-curved platform, the banker blasting under the overall station roof. The C12s also carried out various carriage-pilot duties in and around the North station. Locomotives working on the banking and pilot duties were allocated to New England, while others on branch-line duties were at Spital Bridge depot.

Other veterans at Spital Bridge at this time were five of the GN J52 class 0–6–0 saddle tanks, and seven Great Eastern D16 'Clauds', these 4–4–0s working through to the Midlands among other duties. Rather surprisingly a solitary Great Central J11 was also allocated here, the remaining locomotives being twelve of the powerful J39 class. Visitors to the depot were of many types, including Beyer Garrets, class 5s and the graceful Midland design 2P 4–4–0s, a number of which were employed on Leicester line passenger duties, until more modern motive power in the form of standard designs replaced them in the mid- and late fifties.

New England depot was predominantly a freight depot, with a large number of heavy goods locomotives in its allocation – in the early fifties these were WD 2–8–0s. When the British Railways standard 9F 2–10–0 started to leave the works some of the first were allocated to New England and soon found themselves on heavy coal traffic to Ferme Park, London. Eventually the depot had a considerable number of these locomotives on its books, in addition to the WDs, several of which were gradually transferred away.

Coal traffic on the main line was extensive during the fifties, with a considerable number of trains heading south daily and the corresponding number of empties making their way back to the collieries. New England was also responsible for coal traffic to the power station at Little Barford, just south of St Neots. In 1947 it was decided to transfer a veteran ex-Great Central 2–6–4 tank of class L3, built in 1917, to the depot to work this traffic. This locomotive did not last long on these duties as it was disliked by the enginemen mainly because of braking problems. On occasions, when coming down the bank from Abbots Ripton great consternation was caused if the Huntingdon station signals were against it, or if it was to be turned 'slow road' after passing through the station. In 1950 the L3 returned to Great Central territory and its former depot at Neasden, being withdrawn from service five years later.

Only a small number of passenger locomotives were allocated to New England. These were mainly employed on working some express duties which changed engines at Peterborough, also the semi-fasts to King's Cross and north of Peterborough. In the mid-fifties these were all A2s of various types, including three of the A2s originally built as P2 class 2–8–2s, and subsequently rebuilt to 'Pacific' wheel arrangement: No. 60504 *Mons Meg*, No. 60505 *Thane of Fife* and No. 60506 *Wolf of Badenoch*. When built, the first A2/3, No. 60500 *Edward Thompson*, was allocated to King's Cross, but was later transferred to New England, as was the sole example of the A2/1 to remain in England, No. 60508 *Duke of Rothesay*. Several other A2s were allocated here, one being No. 60533 *Happy Knight*, which was an A2 design fitted with a double chimney. This engine remained at New England for a great many years, and was finally withdrawn from the depot when it closed to steam working.

The Gresley 'maid of all work' the V2 2–6–2 was strongly represented at New England, with a total of thirty-four examples during the early fifties. They were employed on a wide range of duties, including some of the express trains which were worked by 35A locomotives at that time, local passenger traffic and semi-fasts, as well as parcel trains; in addition it was not unusual to see one hauling a heavy coal train, or returning empties. In their last years several members of the class were fitted with double chimneys, considerably altering their appearance. Nos. 60880 and 60881 were among these, and were in their last years New England engines.

Visitors to Peterborough travelling by rail in the fifties could hardly fail to miss the ex-Great Northern J6 0–6–0s which were to be found at all brickyard sidings. The other Great Northern veterans, the J52 saddle tanks, were employed on shunting duties. This class was also very common in the London area at this time. A few of the older J3 and J4 class 0–6–0s still lingered at the depot for a few years after nationalization, mainly finding work on engineering trains and similar light duties. Also in the early days of British Railways K2s and K3s were much in evidence, many being transferred elsewhere on the arrival of classes such as the Ivatt class 4 2–6–0s. Other engines that were allocated here included a Y3 Sentinel which worked in the engineers' yard, and a small number of ex-Great Eastern 0–6–0 tanks which were allocated on shunting duties such as at the Peterborough sugar-beet factory.

At Peterborough North station during the fifties there was a truly fascinating selection of motive power to be seen, with examples of designs originating from the LNER, LMS, Great Northern, Great Central, Great Eastern, Midland and LNWR. Not only could one watch the main-line and local trains, but also locomotives and trains working to and from Peterborough East station, now long since gone. Not surprisingly, Peterborough North usually had a sizeable complement of 'spotters'.

Not many miles away, at March, the massive 500-ton capacity mechanical coaling plant known locally as 'The Wedge', dominated the surrounding flat countryside. At this period March was very much a railway town, with large numbers of its residents working on the railway in some capacity. March depot (shedcode 31B) had an allocation of 164 locomotives in the mid-fifties, comprising mainly freight locomotives. Often this number would be exceeded by the many visitors, some from far afield, which worked into the massive Whitemoor Yards. The hump-shunting yards here once echoed to the sounds of the massive S1 0–8–4 tanks and Q1 0–8–0 tanks as they marshalled trains. By the early fifties, however, they had been transferred away, and the less exciting 0–6–0 diesel shunters had taken over.

March depot covered a large area, being, incidentally, an excellent shed for photography if you were able to gain permission! Like all Eastern and North Eastern Region depots visits were restricted to organized and pre-arranged parties, although one could request individual permission. The depot consisted of two sheds a fair distance apart, the most recent being built in the early thirties and known as the 'wash-out' shed.

Although primarily a freight locomotive depot March had much variety to offer the enthusiast. Apart from the fifteen WD 2–8–0s, a class which seemed to be everywhere in the fifties, a variety of 0–6–0 and 2–6–0 designs were allocated, some of the 0–6–0s going back to Great Eastern days. These included eleven of the J19 class introduced by the Great Eastern in 1912, together with thirteen of the later J20 class introduced in 1920. However, the most interesting were the J17 class veterans, dating back to their introduction by the GER in 1901. They were mainly employed in pick-up and local goods traffic, especially on the branches. The 0–6–0 classes were completed by two Worsdell J15 0–6–0s, sturdy engines in spite of their size; at one time the class was to be found at most of the East Anglian sheds.

March also had a sizeable stock of mixed-traffic locomotives. Principal among these from the early fifties were six Gresley V2 2–6–2s, which found employment on parcels and fast goods trains, many of them to York. The 2–6–0 designs were represented by two classes, numbering in total over a third of the depot's total allocation during the mid-fifties. There were forty-two of the K3 class, originally introduced by the LNER shortly after the grouping, and which were renowned for their rough riding, especially when due for an overhaul. The other 2–6–0 class was the K1, a post-war design which made its appearance in 1949 and twenty-five of which were at March. Naturally, with a shed of this importance, the British Railways standard 9F 2–10–0 soon came on to the scene and replaced some of the depot's existing locomotives. The 9F was to be very much part of the March depot until the end of steam, as even after the depot's steam allocation had finished 9F's still worked in from other depots.

The passenger locomotives at March were of two classes during the fifties, namely eleven of the 'Sandringham' class 4–6–0s and nine of the famous Great Eastern 'Clauds'. The latter 4–4–0s were to be found at many sheds at this time, often working cross-country into regions other than the Eastern. In due course several 'Britannia' class 4–6–2s were allocated to 31B when replaced by diesels elsewhere in East Anglia. Many of these engines were stored in the yard of the 'wash-out' shed. They were suitably protected against the elements and corrosion, and a number later found work elsewhere, several in the London Midland Region, where they were to end their working days.

Tank locomotives were something of a rarity at March, its own allocation consisting of just one or two, usually a J69 0–6–0T, which looked after station duties. Occasionally visiting locomotives would pass through, many on their way to repairs or works overhaul, or returning to their home depot.

As steam was gradually replaced by diesel power a large number of engines were stored in March depot yard, most to make just one more one-way journey! Surprisingly, March is still used for storing withdrawn motive power. A large number of diesels, their working days over, have ended up dumped at March, and at the time of writing many are still standing forlornly in the sidings.

Steam locomotives continued working into March for a while after the depot's own locomotives had finished, many coming from the London Midland Region. Class 5s, 8F 2–8–0s and even 'Jubilee' class 4–6–0s and Stanier class 5MT 2–6–0s were fairly commonplace, as well, of course, as the standard 9F 2–10–0s.

In 1966 the familiar March landmark, 'The Wedge', was demolished. Massive coaling towers were a feature of many locomotive depots. Fortunately, one example still remains to remind us of what was once a most important part of a motive power depot.

The third locomotive depot in the county was Cambridge, having the shedcode 31A. Though not the largest, this was in many ways perhaps the most interesting, having in the early 1950s a large allocation of Great Eastern locomotives including E4 2–4–0s, which were still responsible for passenger duties on several branches and cross-country lines, as also were J15 0–6–0s, several examples of which were fitted with tender cabs for working over the Colne Valley line.

One Cambridge J15, No. 65390, was a regular engine on the first train of the day to Kettering via Huntingdon East. The locomotive would then spend the day at Kettering shed or on shunting duties before returning home with the day's last train back to Cambridge. This particular J15 carried an extra lamp bracket to conform to LMR practice. On occasions other J15s deputized for No. 65390. The 'Claud Hamilton' D16 class 4–4–0s were also very much part of the Cambridge scene. Several were allocated to the depot, while others, usually well maintained mechanically and externally, worked in from other East Anglian sheds. 'Clauds' were to be seen on many services. One turn which took a 31A 'Claud' a long way from home was the Cambridge–Bletchley trains travelling via Sandy and Bedford St John's, the D16 frequently working through to Oxford. For a considerable period No. 62585 was a regular engine for this turn, and could often be seen on Bletchley or Oxford depots looking very out of place in London Midland or Western territory.

Nine 'Sandringhams' were also at Cambridge, including No. 61671 *Royal Sovereign* which was a B2 class locomotive. The engine was employed from time to time on royal trains, when it would be the pride and joy of Cambridge depot. At other times it could be seen on the King's Cross trains. Two other B2s were at the depot, No. 61603 *Framlingham* and No. 61617 *Ford Castle*. The remaining 'Sandringhams' were all B17 class locomotives.

As with most Great Eastern section depots a number of 0–6–0s of various types were allocated. More modern power had arrived by the mid-fifties in the form of Ivatt 2–6–0s, Nos. 46465/6/7, which worked on the Colne Valley line and other branches. B1 class 4–6–0s were beginning to replace 'Sandringhams' on some of the fast turns. Even an Ivatt 4MT 2–6–0 was in allocation early in the fifties.

Veteran tank locomotives which were still at Cambridge at this time found little work, the class F6 2–4–2 tanks occasionally being seen on carriage pilot duties. However, Great Eastern 0–6–0 tanks were active on shunting and pilot duties, aided for a while by ex-Great Northern C12 4–4–2 tanks. Perhaps strangest of all were the three North

Eastern G5 0–4–4 tanks which worked the Bartlow branch and were allocated to Cambridge shed.

The workings of the Cambridge depot could easily be observed from a footbridge which connected the depot to Devonshire Road. To the north of Cambridge station (busy with traffic from both the main line and the long-gone branches) were several locomotive sidings known locally as 'The Dump'. Here could often be found a fascinating variety of engines which included LMR visitors, among which from time to time were LNWR 0–8–0s from Bletchley, engines on their way to and from Stratford works, visitors from other depots, and of course Cambridge-based engines.

A small repair depot was attached to the side of the main locomotive shed. Not far from this point was the reserve coal storage area, for a while a collection of veteran locomotives stood in adjacent sidings. On 22 August 1953 these comprised three F6 2–4–2 tanks, two GNR C12 4–4–2 tanks and four E4 2–4–0s! Only the E4s were to see much service after storage.

Cambridgeshire had three further sub-sheds which came within the county boundary. These were Ely, which usually had three or four engines, all 0–6–0s of the J15 or J17 class. The shed at Huntingdon East was even smaller, with a solitary J15 0–6–0. A small sub-shed also existed at Wisbech and came under March depot's control.

While working on this book I have referred to notes which I made all those years ago, and what fascinating items are to be found in them. There is, for instance, the record of the two preserved Great Northern 'Atlantics' in GNR livery, being run-in prior to a special celebration in September 1953, standing together at the 'Down' slow platform at Huntingdon. They had worked the train from King's Cross and were waiting with the 6.38 p.m. to Peterborough, much to the amazement of many passengers and onlookers. Other unusual visitors included B16 class 4–6–0s from the North Eastern region which made occasional trips south of Peterborough. No. 61461 of York depot was seen heading an empty stock train north on 14 September 1953, and No. 61453 of the same depot was on a similar turn on 24 December 1953, while a very clean member of the class, No. 61444 was seen in the county on a fast goods on 28 January 1954.

'Pacifics' could occasionally be seen on strange turns, even southbound coal trains! On 26 April 1954 the now preserved A4 No. 60009 *Union of South Africa* of Haymarket depot, Edinburgh, worked a fast fitted goods north. Other strange workings in the area included, on 19 October 1954, Ivatt 2–6–0 No. 46482 of West Auckland shed, working south light engine and, on 9 January 1955, A2 class, No. 60531 *Bahram*, of Aberdeen Ferryhill depot. Indeed, Scottish area 'Pacifics' would often be seen south of Peterborough on running-in turns ex-Doncaster works. One of these turns was regularly the 'Doncaster parcels', which arrived at Huntingdon at approximately 1.30 a.m. Locomotives from many depots worked this turn.

Tank locomotives from the London area depots were often worked (usually overnight) light engine to Doncaster and returned after overhaul in the same manner. As the fifties progressed many of the engines which worked north never returned. Locomotives of classes J50 and J52, and 0–6–2 tanks of N1 and N2 were mostly overhauled at Doncaster, many also ending their days there.

Several unusual locomotives were to be seen on special trains after steam had finished on the main line, mostly taking over the train at Peterborough. Two such were 'Castle' class No. 7029 *Clun Castle*, which worked a 'Silver Jubilee Special' on 8 October 1967, and a Western Region 'Britannia', No. 70020 *Mercury*. The preserved A4, No. 4498 *Sir Nigel Gresley*, and A3, No. 4472 *Flying Scotsman*, both took part in special workings, the latter working to and from London with two tenders.

Within the pages of the book is a representative selection of what was to be seen on Cambridgeshire rails in the period from 1950 to the very end of steam workings, revealing the wealth of locomotive designs which were active within the county during this period, and depicting the 'swan song' of the steam locomotive in the county of Cambridgeshire.

THE LAST DAYS OF STEAM IN
CAMBRIDGESHIRE

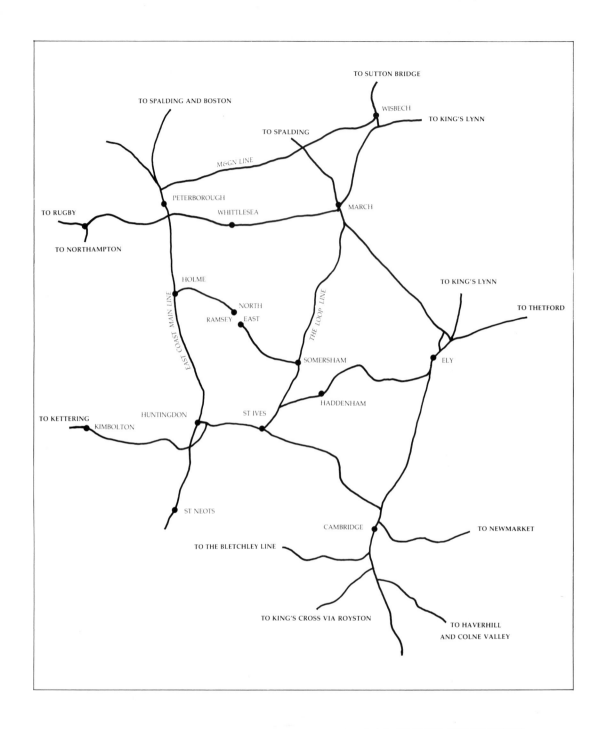

THE LAST DAYS OF STEAM IN CAMBRIDGESHIRE
Only locations relevant to the text are shown

The East Coast Main Line
South of Peterborough

Immingham depot had several B1s on its allocation during the 1950s. One important turn that the locomotives worked was the daily express to King's Cross. Here No. 61142 starts away from Huntingdon on the long climb to Abbots Ripton with the return evening working.

8.6.57

V2 No. 60906 rejoins the 'Up' main line at Abbots Ripton. Looking at this location now it would be difficult to believe that there had ever been a station.

3.10.53

A3 No. 60044 *Melton* in its final days of service nears the end of the long 1:200 climb from Huntingdon. After withdrawal *Melton* was stored at New England depot for a while, before going to Doncaster works for scrapping.

5.5.63

For a few months 'Britannia' class locomotives worked the King's Cross to Cleethorpes service, having taken over the working from B1s. No. 70040 *Clive of India* leaves Huntingdon with the northbound train in fine style.

9.61

Another view of *Clive of India* on the Cleethorpes service, the engine making light work of the ten-coach train, as it has steam to spare.

9.61

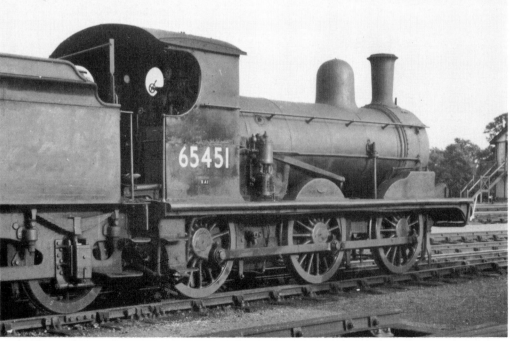

This photograph of J15 No. 65451 shows the open cab fitted to these locomotives. Note the Westinghouse brake. J15s were powerful locomotives for their size.

This photograph shows J15 No. 65420 while Huntingdon pilot; it was later to be the last J15 at Huntingdon, as it was the engine used on track lifting on the Huntingdon to St Ives line. Huntingdon East station can be seen on the right-hand side of the picture. The old water-storage tank at the North station is on the left.

A4 No. 60026 *Miles Beevor* pulls smartly away from Huntingdon with a King's Cross express. Note the sidings and well-used goods yard which existed at that time.

18.3.55

A4 *Dwight D. Eisenhower* makes an impressive start from Huntingdon. This A4 is one of the six preserved, two of which are now overseas, No. 60008 being preserved in the United States.

This rather strange sight was seen at Huntingdon in September 1961, as an unidentified WD and J15 No. 65420 headed back to New England depot for servicing. The J15 was employed on lifting track on the St Ives–Huntingdon section at the time.

21.9.61

New England J6 class 0–6–0s were frequently used for working engineering trains. No. 64224 is here seen on such a working at Huntingdon. Note the six-wheeled coach.

9.5.54

A4 No. 60031 *Golden Plover* of Haymarket depot, Edinburgh, heads the non-stop 'Elizabethan' near Huntingdon. This prestige turn was shared by Haymarket and King's Cross A4s.

26.8.54

For a number of years a pick-up goods was operated to and from Huntingdon worked by a Hitchin depot locomotive. L1 2–6–4T No. 67744 here awaits the time for its return south. Note the wagon-loading gauge.

17.9.54

Only one stopping train ran from Peterborough to King's Cross on a Sunday morning in the early fifties. The turn was usually worked by a New England B1 or A2/2 'Pacific'. B1 No. 61330 was on the duty when the this photograph was taken as it leaves Huntingdon.

28.9.52

Three of these A2/2 'Pacifics' were allocated to New England, the other three being York engines. No. 60506 *Wolf of Badenoch* pulls smartly away with a King's Cross train, albeit amid much leaking steam.

The Huntingdon pilot was always a J15 0–6–0 from Cambridge depot. No. 65442 stands in the yards after having recently received a general works overhaul.

25.8.54

Evening shadows lengthen as B1 No. 61331 leaves Huntingdon with a King's Cross to Peterborough train. B1s were seen on passenger, parcels and fast goods trains. A regular southbound fish train ran in the early evening and usually had a B1 in charge.

A4 No. 60022 *Mallard* seen here at Huntingdon working a King's Cross to Edinburgh train in June 1955. The rail strike at the time meant that very few trains were running.

5.6.55

In the last days of steam south of Peterborough, New England A3s often found themselves relegated to local passenger workings. No. 60050 *Persimmon* is here heading the afternoon King's Cross to Peterborough.

28.3.63

This rather unusual photograph shows No. 60800 *Green Arrow* on a northbound pick-up goods and No. 60500 *Edward Thompson* on the afternoon King's Cross–Peterborough semi-fast passenger train, photographed at Huntingdon.

29.7.52

V2 No. 60832 heads for London with a heavy coal train. V2s were not usual on these workings, the normal motive power being New England standard 9F 2–10–0s or WD 2–8–0s. However, on occasions such as this any locomotive available would be used, even 'Pacifics'.

A3 No. 60046 *Diamond Jubilee* makes easy work of the Hull express. The A3 had been fitted with a double chimney, but had not yet received smoke deflectors. On the right is the third set of 'Down' line TPO despatching apparatus.

6.7.59

A2 No. 60533 *Happy Knight* is seen here at Huntingdon in a very run-down condition. The locomotive was working the Sunday morning King's Cross to Peterborough local train.

21.4.63

J50 No. 68991 takes water at Huntingdon as it works north on its final journey to Doncaster. The J50 class was a very familiar sight in the London area for a great many years.

The unique W1 4–6–4 No. 60700 was a regular engine on the East Coast Main Line. In this photograph it is seen leaving Huntingdon with a Sunday local passenger service to Peterborough.
14.8.52

A platelayer walks by unconcerned as W1 4–6–4 No. 60700 thunders by at the head of a York express. The W1 was a familiar sight for many years on the East Coast Main Line.

3.5.56

A3 No. 60050 *Persimmon* stands at Huntingdon as V2 No. 60948 heads north on the 'Down' slow with a train of flat wagons.

28.3.63

A1 No. 60136 *Alcazar* stands at Huntingdon while working a King's Cross to Peterborough local service. *Alcazar* was a Grantham engine at the time and would be working back to its home depot.

7.8.52

9F 2–10–0 No. 92040 has been given the main line at Huntingdon as it heads a long train of empties north. The engine is getting to grips with the climb to Abbots Ripton.

Looking at this photograph of A3 No. 60102 *Sir Frederick Banbury*, it is difficult to believe the locomotive was withdrawn the following month, in October 1961. The A3 has received a double chimney but is without smoke deflectors.

14.9.61

The famous *Mallard*, No. 60022, again, photographed at the head of a local passenger train. King's Cross 'Pacifics' often filled in on turns such as this.

4.7.54

Isinglass, in the A3's final form, heads a local train at Huntingdon. No. 60063 was a King's Cross engine. The smokebox shows signs of hard work!

14.4.63

A rare visitor to the East Coast Main Line, No. 70000 *Britannia*, is seen heading north with a fast goods. The engine was allocated to March at the time; only on very rare occasions were 31B engines seen south of Peterborough.

9.61

J15 No. 65390 shunts oil tanks through Huntingdon North. In the background, under the cycle shelter, are a number of pigeon boxes, once a familiar sight on the railways.

3.5.56

The train waits on the 'Down' slow line. A small oil depot was situated at the northern end of Huntingdon station.

V2 No. 60800 *Green Arrow* was a King's Cross engine for many years. Here the locomotive carries out shunting duties at Huntingdon while in charge of a northbound goods.

29.7.52

A2/3 No. 60513 *Dante*, a New England engine, leaves Huntingdon with the 9.39 a.m. to King's Cross. Note the unusual signal indicating the trains will run slow road, for so many years a feature at Huntingdon.

9.5.54

V2 No. 60904 stands at Huntingdon at the head of a King's Cross to Peterborough semi-fast. V2s were very common on the East Coast Main Line, often not getting a second glance. How different it would be now!

28.9.52

A rare visitor, A3 No. 60083 *Sir Hugo*, heads north from Huntingdon on the slow line. It is fitted with double chimney and German-type smoke deflectors.

3.3.63

L1 2–6–4 tanks were common on the East Coast Main Line for a number of years. No. 67746 is seen here leaving Huntingdon.

16.7.54

A V2 in trouble at Huntingdon: steam envelopes the front end of No. 60842 as it attempts to start away from Huntingdon.

24.5.53

V2 No. 60956 departs from Huntingdon North with the 9.39 a.m. to King's Cross. Locomotives employed on this duty ranged from A3s and A4s to V2s, as here. No. 60956 was a Doncaster engine and in green livery when this photograph was taken.

22.4.57

One of the last Great Northern somersault signals was this fine example on the 'Up' lines at Great Paxton, near St Neots. This photograph shows to the right the long since demolished Paxton signal-box.

6.53

V2 No. 60845 photographed at St Neots as it heads north with a container train. 'Pacifics' and V2s shared fast goods workings.

12.8.54 (Photograph: Alan Blencowe)

B1 No. 61079 on the King's Cross to Cleethorpes express passes St Neots. This train made its first stop at Huntingdon.

21.8.56 (Photograph: Alan Blencowe)

B16 No. 61468, a visitor from the North Eastern Region, seen here heading north with a fast goods at St Neots. B16s were not common south of Peterborough.

23.8.56 (Photograph: Alan Blencowe)

A3 No. 60103 *Flying Scotsman* approaches St Neots with an 'Up' express. This famous A3 was a regular sight on the main line at this time; for a considerable number of years it was on the Great Central line.

12.8.54 (Photograph: Alan Blencowe)

Peterborough and Area

The scene at the north end of Peterborough station. V2 No. 60912 starts out at the head of a northbound express.

9.53

A locomotive stabling-point was to be found at the north end of Peterborough station. It was usual for a passenger locomotive to stand by for failures. Here V2 No. 60880 awaits a call. This V2 was one of those fitted with a double chimney. The locomotive remained in service until September 1963, when it was withdrawn from Doncaster shed, ending its days at the works.

6.9.62

Frequently heavy trains at Peterborough North would slip badly: the start was made difficult by the curve in the station platform. Almost invariably a C12 4–4–2 tank would have to assist at the rear. Here No. 67368 stands ready for the big push.

5.2.53

K2 No. 61731 of Boston depot arrives at Peterborough. Twelve K2s were allocated to Boston depot in the mid-fifties.

7.8.54

Several C12 4–4–2 tanks were allocated to New England depot. Their duties included carriage pilot, banker and several branch-line duties. No. 67365 here brings in stock to Peterborough North. Note the large dome which was fitted to the C12s.

5.9.53

King's Cross depot V2 No. 60914 arrives at Peterborough at the head of a relief express. Eleven V2s were allocated to King's Cross at this time with New England having twenty-three members of the class.

5.9.53

Class 2P 4–4–0 No. 40485 stands at Peterborough East station. Services to Rugby and Northampton operated from this station in addition to the East Anglian services.

5.2.53

A King's Cross to Leeds express photographed north of Peterborough behind A1 No. 60148 *Aboyeur* of Grantham depot.

The southbound 'Northumbrian' approaches Walton crossing behind V2 No. 60928. V2s were often found in charge of heavy express trains. Note the 'travelling post office' lineside apparatus.

The southbound 'Flying Scotsman', with No. 60014 *Silver Link* of King's Cross depot in charge, seen on the approaches to Peterborough.

26.9.55

Immingham depot always maintained its B1 class locomotives in superb condition during the 1950s. B1 No. 61079 was no exception. It is here seen arriving at Peterborough.

4.12.54

V2 No. 60975 restarts a King's Cross to Edinburgh express at Peterborough. At this time V2s were often to be found in charge of express trains. Note the end-of-platform water-crane and heating-stove.

5.9.53

Silver Fox makes a spirited start from Peterborough. No. 60017 carried a fox emblem on its side.
14.8.54

V2 No. 60874 passes Walton crossing in fine style with a northbound express which it had just taken over at Peterborough.

A1 No. 60116 *Hal o' the Wynd* heads the northbound 'Heart of Midlothian' towards Walton crossing. On the right-hand side of the picture can be seen the Leicester line.

24.9.55

V2 No. 60936 makes easy going of a four-coach northbound local passenger train.

24.9.55

J67/1 No. 68496 assisting in shunting operations at Peterborough sugar-beet factory. Considerable traffic was handled here by rail, especially during the height of the season.

4.12.54

J6 No. 64211 heads a lightweight pick-up goods northbound. The J6 class was a very successful design introduced by Gresley for the Great Northern Railway in 1911.

24.9.55

A4 No. 60011 *Empire of India* of Haymarket depot whistles to warn of its approach to Peterborough station at the head of the southbound 'Elizabethan'. Until the station was rebuilt all express trains ran through the station on a speed restriction.

5.9.53

A3 No. 60108 *Gay Crusader* has shut off steam for the approach to Peterborough at Walton crossing. Note the line indicators on the pole on the left of the picture.

Heavy southbound coal trains were a very common sight north of Peterborough. Here O4/3 No. 63717 ambles south. This locomotive was rebuilt to class O4/8 in March 1958, remaining in service until 1965.

24.9.55

Another photograph of No. 63717 as it heads a coal train south. The engine had recently received a works overhaul and was making light work of its heavy load.

O2 No. 63982 heads a train of flat wagons north from Peterborough. This class was introduced in 1921. No. 63982 was an O2/3, a development with a side-window cab and reduced boiler mountings.

The rather spartan station building on the March line at Whittlesea. Note the amount of sidings still to be found at country stations in the 1950s.

9.9.56

Whittlesea station as it was in the autumn of 1956. This view, looking towards March, reveals a wealth of railway items, including the gas-lights, signal-box and trackwork as well as the interesting signal which announces the arrival of a train for the Peterborough direction.

9.9.56

D16/3 No. 62605 heads a motley twelve-vehicle collection of parcel vans and wagons at Whittlesea station. The 'Claud' was at this time a Cambridge engine.

9.9.56

4F No. 44113 heads a heavy coal train on the Leicester line. The train is nearing Walton crossing on its way to Peterborough.

24.9.55

The 2P class 4–4–0s were regular engines on the Leicester line for a number of years. No. 40526 is seen in fine form near Walton. Many of the services on this line were later to be handled by standard class 4MTs.

Another 2P, No. 40453, trundles along the Leicester line near Walton with a local passenger train. This 2P was allocated to Burton 17B.

24.9.55

The 35A and 35C C12 4–4–2 tanks which were employed on branch-line duties always returned to Peterborough for servicing. No. 67368 here ambles along the Leicester line on its way to Spital Bridge depot.

24.9.55

The main station building at Ramsey North, with several wagons still in various parts of the yard.
7.55

Another view of Ramsey North. Ramsey had two branches serving the town: the Great Northern branch from Holme on the main line and the Great Eastern branch from Somersham on the St Ives–March line. Ramsey North was the terminus of the old GNR branch.

7.55

Cambridge, March and Eastern Cambridgeshire

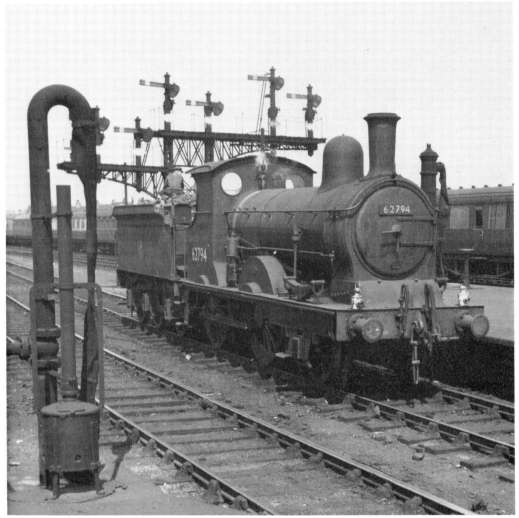

E4 class No. 62794 at Cambridge. In the background are some interesting signals while the water-cranes, and the attendant heating unit visible on the near side, are reminders of days now long gone.

13.7.54

Unfortunately no examples of the 'Claud Hamilton' class have been preserved. These engines were for many years part of the East Anglian scene. Here D16/3 No. 62576 awaits the signal to proceed on shed. This engine was one of those rebuilt with round-topped boiler and modified footplating.

9.5.55

B2 class No. 61671 *Royal Sovereign* awaits departure from Cambridge at the head of a King's Cross train. This locomotive was often employed on the King's Cross roster, except when called upon for royal duties.

17.5.52

'Sandringham' class No. 61642 *Kilverstone Hall* was one of the class allocated to 31A. It is seen here at the head of a local passenger train at Cambridge station.

15.9.51

The now preserved E4 No. 62785 is awaiting departure from Cambridge for Mildenhall. Note the veteran carriages in the background. During its last years in service this E4 spent a short time at Hitchin depot for use on the Henlow branch.

15.9.51

L1 No. 67730 of Stratford shed stands in the bay platform at Cambridge. Thompson L1 2–6–4 tanks were frequently seen at Cambridge at this time.

13.7.54

'Britannia' class No. 70002 *Geoffrey Chaucer* takes water at the north end of Cambridge station, and at the same time gives the footplatemen a chance of a breather.

10.10.55

March depot had eleven 'Sandringhams' in its allocation, including B17/6 No. 61627 *Aske Hall*, photographed here in the north bay at Cambridge. Behind it is the side wall of the motive power depot.

10.10.55

2MT No. 46401 heads a Kettering train about to leave Cambridge. The locomotive depot can be seen in the background.

16.8.51

Repairs to Sentinel Y3 class, Departmental No. 42, were carried out at Chesterton permanent-way depot, seen here in Autumn 1955.

10.10.55

Back in service again No. 42 was on shunting duties at Chesterton in 1957. The enclosed cabs of these locomotives must have made them unbearingly hot at this time of year.

23.6.57

E4 class locomotives were known as 'Intermediates'. No. 62796, here photographed at Cambridge, was coupled to a back cab tender at this time. No. 62796 was to remain in service for a further eighteen months.

10.10.55

2–6–4 tanks of Stanier and Fairburn designs were employed on the Bletchley to Cambridge service until replaced by standard class 4 tanks. Here No. 80082 heads the Bletchley train.

9.5.55

D16/3 No. 62618, one of the two 'Clauds' which were used for royal train working, stands at Cambridge. Note the smart appearance of the engine and the burnished steel ring on the smokebox door. This engine and No. 62614, the other royal engine, were restored to LNER green livery shortly after the war, being repainted in British Railways black lined-out livery in the early fifties.

17.5.52

Though Departmental No. 42 spent most of its time at Chesterton permanent-way depot, on occasions it was seen at the small engineers' yard near the locomotive depot, where this photograph was taken.

2.8.55

B2 No. 61603 *Framlingham* heads a Liverpool Street train at Cambridge. This engine was withdrawn in 1958 with the other 31A B2s, Nos. 61617 and 61671.

2.8.57

After the early fifties the F6 tanks at Cambridge were not often seen in use. No. 67237 was carriage pilot when this photograph was taken.

16.8.51

D16 No. 62589 is seen leaving Cambridge station with a heavy passenger train on a rather grey April day in 1955. 'Clauds' were responsible for express trains such as the 'Fenman' at this time.

B17/6 No. 61635 *Milton* stands ready to leave Cambridge and work back to its home depot of March. The wall on the right-hand side is that of the locomotive depot. The B17/6 locomotives were fitted with 100A (B1 type) boilers.

31.5.56

E4 No. 62784 heads a Cambridgeshire branch-train in the early fifties. The engine is seen running with a 'water-cart' tender. No. 62784 was withdrawn in May 1955.
(Photograph: Author's Collection)

The decrepit station building at Ramsey East only occasionally saw passenger traffic in the fifties, when one or two special excursions ran from the East station to Yarmouth races. In 1955, when the photograph was taken, however, a reasonable amount of goods traffic still used the branch.

The guard opens the gates for J19 No. 64641 at Warboys on the branch from Somersham to Ramsey East.

25.4.55 (Photograph: Alan Blencowe)

The daily goods train on the Ramsey East branch was usually lightly loaded. Here J17 No. 65587 has only the brake-van for its journey from Ramsey East.

1.2.55 (Photograph: Alan Blencowe)

March J17s worked pick-up goods on both the main line and branches. No. 65538 is here photographed at Chatteris.

22.10.56 (Photograph: Alan Blencowe)

K1 No. 62018 busies itself with shunting operations in Chatteris goods yard. This pick-up goods was very much part of the Cambridgeshire railway scene in the fifties.

27.9.55 (Photograph: Alan Blencowe)

D16/3 No. 62559 runs into Chatteris with a Cambridge passenger train. 'Clauds' handled most of these runs, though occasionally a 'Sandringham' would appear.

6.10.55 (Photograph: Alan Blencowe)

D16/3 No. 62618 at Chatteris station the head of a Cambridge train. Both the 'royal' ' Clauds' were regular engines on the March–Cambridge service.

26.2.55 (Photograph: Alan Blencowe)

O1 class No. 63650 trundles through Chatteris station with an 'Up' freight. A considerable number of goods trains used the 'loop line' daily.

(Photograph: Alan Blencowe)

K3 No. 61842, at the head of an 'Up' local passenger train, passes the distinctive station buildings at Manea.

13.3.54 (Photograph: Alan Blencowe)

J68 No. 68664 was on station-pilot duties at March when this photograph was taken. Note the unusual station roof in the background. Only one or two tank locomotives were allocated to March.

8.11.52

D16/3 No. 62539 pulls smartly away from March with a local passenger train. This was a March engine, nine members of the class being allocated to the depot.

8.11.52

D16/3 No. 62530 makes a spirited start from Wisbech on a grey and rainy day. This 'Claud' was a Cambridge engine during the early fifties.

(Photograph: R.K. Blencowe collection)

B12 No. 61516 at Wisbech. Judging from the individuals watching, the train might have been a rail tour.

(Photograph: R.K. Blencowe collection)

D16/3 No. 62570 waits at Ely station ready to take over a train for King's Lynn.
10.4.54 (Photograph: Alan Blencowe)

J17 No. 65587 seen here on the approach to Ely with an 'Up' freight. Several members of this class
were usually sub-shedded at Ely.

(Photograph: Alan Blencowe)

Huntingdon East and St Ives

J15 No. 65477 fills up at Huntingdon East before working the afternoon goods to St Ives and back.
Note the fine footbridge.

The view from Huntingdon East station. Note the check rails, locomotive depot, and water-crane. On the far right is the Cambridge to Kettering line, both lines in the foreground connecting to the East Coast Main Line.

25.12.55

Huntingdon shed was located in a spot over which the present-day bypass has been built. This photograph shows J15 No. 65474 over the ashpit. Behind the engine was the small turntable. The single-road shed was seldom used, as almost invariably the engine would stand outside.

6.2.55

In the fruit season a special train ran from the Cambridgeshire fruit-growing districts over the branch to Kettering. The engine had to struggle unaided to Huntingdon East due to severe weight restrictions on the numerous wooden trestle bridges. A pilot was attached at Huntingdon East to assist over the hilly section. No. 46400 stands waiting for the train after having worked in light engine.

2MT No. 46444 meanders along with the afternoon train three years before the branch was closed. This photograph was taken on the section between Buckden and Huntingdon East.

2.4.56

2MT No. 46400 calls at Buckden station on its way to Cambridge. The signal-box is now preserved at another site, having been used as a greenhouse for several years after the branch closed.

2F No. 58214 at the head of the Kettering pick-up goods stands unusually in Huntingdon East station. In order to regain the Kettering line the train would have to set back.

J15 No. 65451 rattles round the curve to Huntingdon East with a transfer freight from St Ives. The wagons would be sorted at Huntingdon, and despatched north or south as required.

3.3.55

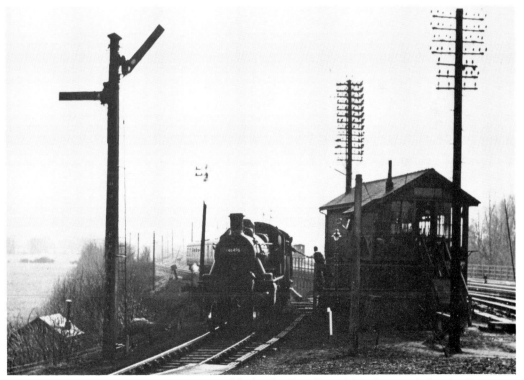

Huntingdon No. 1 signal-box was responsible for the East Coast Main Line and also the Kettering to Cambridge branch. Here No. 46496 exchanges the 'token' with the signalman as it enters Huntingdon East station. Note the unusual two-way signal.

The afternoon train to Cambridge is seen leaving Huntingdon East. These 2MTs were the largest locomotives permitted over the section from Kimbolton to St Ives due to the weight restrictions already mentioned, which were particularly severe in the Huntingdon and St Ives area.

No. 46444 seen between Grafham and Huntingdon at the head of a Cambridge train. The train has already crossed under the East Coast Main Line and is preparing to attack the incline to the East station.

15.3.55

Every weekday a pick-up goods ran from Kettering to Godmanchester. In the early fifties this was worked by ex-Midland Railway 2F 0–6–0s. When Kettering depot received additional Ivatt 2MTs, the duty was handed over. Here No. 46496 stands in Huntingdon East station before working back to Kettering.

17.6.52

The lightweight afternoon goods for St Ives leaves Huntingdon East behind J15 No. 65475, passing the engine shed. Usually the return working would consist of twenty or more wagons for forwarding north or south from Huntingdon.

4.10.52

Very occasionally, if Cambridge depot was short of J15s, one from another shed within the district would appear as Huntingdon pilot. This was the case here when No. 65391 of Bury St Edmunds is seen on the duty.

9.51

J15 No. 65477 arrives at Huntingdon with the return goods working from St Ives. Considerable interchange took place during the fifties between St Ives and Huntingdon.

25.5.54

2MT No. 46496 crosses the River Ouse at Huntingdon with the midday Cambridge to Kettering train. The first five of the 2MT class built were allocated new to Kettering, and commenced working the Cambridge service upon arrival. The ageing Midland 2Fs which they succeeded had themselves taken over from MR 2–4–0s.

Huntingdon East locomotive depot with J15 No. 65461 'on shed'. It was very rare for more than one locomotive to be found here. Over many years I can only ever recall one such occasion, when two were present at one time, one of these being an E4 2–4–0 which had failed.

J15 No. 65477 stands by over the ashpit at the coal stage at Huntingdon.

7.8.52

J15 No. 65461 at Huntingdon depot. On the adjacent line loco coal has been delivered. The wagon nearest the shed shows traces of its one-time private ownership.

14.8.52

Huntingdon East depot had a small turntable at the rear of the shed building. The only engines to use this on a regular basis were the 2F 0–6–0s and later the 2MT 2–6–0s of Kettering depot. 2F No. 58214 here makes heavy going for the crew.

J6 No. 64186 stands in Huntingdon East. This locomotive would not be permitted to work past the locomotive depot due to the severe curves and weight restrictions.

12.5.55

Mention of J15 No. 65390 working the Cambridge to Kettering service has already been made. Here the locomotive heads for its home depot near Mill Common, crossing with the last train of the day from Kettering.

5.7.54

The J15 class 0–6–0s had a surprising turn of speed when working passenger trains. In their heyday they would often be employed on excursion traffic. No. 65390 had worked through from Kettering and is seen here leaving Godmanchester.

25.5.54

2MT No. 46465 worked over the Cambridge–Kettering line for a short period. This picture of the engine was taken at Godmanchester. Note the wagons and the mill in the background.

18.7.51

No. 46401 was a regular engine on the Kettering–Cambridge line. When these sturdy 2MT locomotives arrived they considerably improved the service. Their cabs were also a great deal better than the open ones of the Midland 0–6–0s. No. 46401 was photographed leaving Huntingdon East.

Track-lifting of the St Ives–Huntingdon section had reached Godmanchester by the end of August 1961. J15 No. 65420 was in charge of the train. The J15 travelled to and from New England daily while working on this duty.

J15 No. 65420 stands on one of the many wooden trestle bridges on the Huntingdon–St Ives section while in charge of the track-lifting train. Godmanchester Mill is in the background.

The train of lifted track stands over the level crossing at Godmanchester while chains are adjusted. Godmanchester Mill can again be seen in the background.

2MT No. 46401 awaits the 'right away' for Cambridge outside St Ives Junction signal-box. Only three trains ran each way on weekdays from Kettering to Cambridge, with no Sunday service.
17.4.51

An unusual photograph of D16/3 No. 62618, one of the two 'royal' 'Clauds'. This engine and No.
62614 both received LNER green livery in 1949. No. 62618 is here photographed in green livery at
St Ives six months before it was repainted in British Railways lined black in October 1951.

17.4.51

Ivatt 2MT No. 46400 joins the March to Cambridge line at St Ives station on the afternoon train
from Kettering. Two standard 2MTs Nos. 78020 and 78021, were allocated to 15B in addition to the
Ivatt 2–6–0s.

23.5.53

St Ives Junction signal-box has given the 'road' to standard class 2MT No. 78020 at the head of the afternoon train.

25.8.54

Station staff at St Ives busy themselves with the afternoon parcels train while the driver takes a few minutes to pose against B17/1 No. 61619 *Welbeck Abbey* of March depot. The engine was working back to its home depot when this photograph was taken.

8.9.54

D16/3 62569 of King's Lynn depot awaits the 'right away' from St Ives with a Cambridge train. Note the white headcode carried by the locomotive. Next to the engine is a vintage six-wheeled brake-van.

1.7.54

The Cambridge to March line via St Ives was known as the 'loop line'. A large number of freight trains worked over the route daily. Here WD No. 90064 heads for March with a train of empties.
23.5.53

The afternoon passenger train to Cambridge leaves St Ives behind D16/3 No. 62618, one of the two 'Clauds' used for royal duties. The engine had by the time this photograph was taken been repainted in standard BR black lined livery.

23.5.53

WD No. 90442 rattles through St Ives with a heavy goods. As can be seen, the station was on a quite sharp curve.

23.5.53

A grimy J17, No. 65554, trundles through St Ives on its way to March. J17s were often seen at St Ives on duties such as this, together with K1s, WDs and others.

23.5.53

No. 62020, one of March depot's numerous K1 2–6–0s, heads past St Ives for home base with a mixed goods.

17.3.54

A long train of coal empties makes J19 0–6–0 No. 64650 work hard round the curves at St Ives. Normally this traffic was handled by WDs or K1s.

17.3.54

D16/3 No. 62614, one of the two 'royal' 'Clauds', approaches St Ives with a lightweight Cambridge train. No. 62614 was a King's Lynn engine at this time.

17.3.54

No. 62614 drifts into St Ives with a March train. Most of the passenger traffic over the 'loop' was worked by 'Clauds' and occasionally 'Sandringhams'.

24.6.54

Mishaps and Incidents

L1 2–6–4T No. 67740 has been derailed on a crossover just north of Huntingdon North station, completely disrupting services on the East Coast Main Line. Here the New England breakdown crane commences re-railing the locomotive.

19.5.51

This veteran J3 class 0–6–0, No. 64116, has come off the rails in Huntingdon and awaits the attention of the New England crane. Note the lettering 'British Railways' still on the tender. In their later years the few remaining J3s and J4s worked engineering trains and short-trip workings.
10.6.51

On this occasion the Huntingdon pilot, J15 No. 65475 became derailed near the East station locomotive shed while working the St Ives goods. Preparing for re-railing to commence, a young fireman has been placed on the J15, which has a fair head of steam.
3.8.55

The 45 ton New England breakdown crane arrives and is shunted into position by WD No. 90519. This was remarkable in itself, as the locomotive would have had to pass through the East station with its very tight radius curves or platform clearances. Note the vintage coach in use at this time with the crane set.

The crane sets to work to put things right, dealing first with a derailed van. The maximum lift on the crane jib was 36 tons. Breakdown cranes were usually maintained in 'light steam' at their home depots, which were principal locomotive depots. By the time they arrived on site steam would be at working pressure, and work could commence immediately.

This photograph shows the New England crane at work on No. 65475, the tender having been raised and made ready for re-railing. The whole procedure is being watched over carefully by the locomotive men from New England in charge of the operation.

The New England breakdown crane is here seen in action again, this time on a northbound fast goods which had come to grief at Offord headed by A1 No. 60123 *H.A. Ivatt*. Some of the vans have been reduced to little more than firewood.

8.9.62

H.A. Ivatt was moved into sidings at Offord the following day, where it was photographed prior to removal to Doncaster works. The engine was condemned following this incident – steam locomotives were being rapidly withdrawn at this time – and was cut up at Doncaster in October 1962. Note the marks on the boiler caused by chains during the lifting operation.

Special Trains and Excursions

New England B1 No. 61391 photographed at Whittlesea heading the second RCTS 'Fensman' rail tour. Passengers are alighting to join a train of open wagons for a trip over the Benwick branch.
9.9.56

J15 No. 65562 with open wagons and brake vans either end ready to work the enthusiasts' special over the Benwick branch. This particular J15, one of several allocated to March depot, was used on several specials around this time.

9.9.56

J15 No. 65474 heads a five-coach excursion train to Yarmouth races. The train is seen here arriving at Bluntisham station.

16.9.53 (Photograph: author's collection)

A3 No. 60103 *Flying Scotsman* heads north near Huntingdon with a Westminster Bank Railway Society special to York. *Flying Scotsman* was a Grantham engine at this time.

3.4.55

The two preserved Great Northern 'Atlantics' seen near Abbots Ripton as they head south with the 'Plant Centenarian'. The C2 No. 990 *Henry Oakley* is piloting C1 No. 251; both had been withdrawn and preserved for some years, the C2 having been withdrawn in 1937.

27.9.53

J17 No. 65562 crosses the Fens near Warboys on its way to Ramsey East with the first RCTS 'Fensman' special.

24.7.55

The 'Fensman' after its arrival at Ramsey East station. J17 No. 65562 was one of the few J17s to be vacuum-fitted.

24.7.55

The 'Fensman' heads back along the branch to Somersham where it would connect with the 'loop line' from March to Cambridge via St Ives.

24.7.55

Locomotive men gather round A3 No. 60106 *Flying Fox* at Peterborough while it takes on water. The A3 was working the 'London North Eastern Flier', a special on which the A3 made a superb run.

2.5.64

A4, No. 60009 *Union of South Africa* leaves Peterborough at the head of the combined RCTS and SLS 'Jubilee Requiem' to Newcastle.

24.10.64

On a misty morning 'Britannia' class No. 70020 *Mercury* photographed at Peterborough while working a 'Home Counties Railway Society' train to York.

4.10.64

Castle class No. 7029 *Clun Castle* was prepared at New England in October 1967 before working the Ian Allan 'Silver Jubilee' special to York.

8.10.67

In the same month another preserved locomotive which visited Peterborough to work a special north was A4 No. 4498 *Sir Nigel Gresley*, seen here moving off New England depot.

1.10.67

No. 4472 *Flying Scotsman*, restored to its original LNER livery and number, leaves Peterborough with the 'White Rose' special to York.

1.5.66

Flying Scotsman heads north near Abbots Ripton with the 'Michelangelo Tour' in April 1967, several years after steam had finished on this section. Note the two tenders which the locomotive ran with at this time.

30.4.67

New England and Spital Bridge
Locomotive Depots

A3 No. 60062 *Minoru* receives attention in the repair shop at New England. In the last months of steam at the depot several A3s were on the allocation.

6.12.64

Ivatt 2MT 2–6–0s were widely used in North Norfolk. Here No. 43063 is photographed at New England depot. The tablet exchange apparatus can be clearly seen on the tender.

Three of these A2/2 class 'Pacifics' were allocated to New England, the other three being at York. This 1955 photograph is of No. 60504 *Mons Meg*. The other two 35A locos were *Thane of Fife* and *Wolf of Badenoch*. The A2/2s were rebuilds of Gresley P2 class 2–8–2s, rebuilding having taken place in 1943/4.

WD 2–8–0s were so common in the county that no one took any notice of them. How different it would be now! No. 90349 is here on shed at 35A.

13.5.55

A class that was to be associated with New England for many years was the standard class 9F 2–10–0. Several 9Fs were still on allocation when the depot closed to steam. The engine photographed here is No. 92042.

Standard class 4MT No. 76046 was just ex-works and on running-in turn, when photographed at New England. Note the high running-plate on these locomotives. In the background is one of the depots many J52 0–6–0 saddle tanks.

One of the dirtiest jobs at a motive power depot was clearing and working in the ashpits. Two members of New England depot's staff attend B1 No. 61210, a 35A engine.

13.5.55

In the early fifties over thirty of these interesting ex-Great Northern C12 4–4–2 tanks were in service, several members of the class being in the Peterborough area. No. 67352 was one of these, seen here at New England.

J52 class No. 68817 was engaged in supplying steam for boiler wash-outs at New England.

Two tank locomotives can here be seen stored in the shed yard at New England, C12 4–4–2 tank No. 67366 and a J52 0–6–0ST. The chimneys have been covered. In the case of No. 67366, however, it was to see further service, remaining in stock until withdrawn in April 1958.

13.5.55

In the fifties one could not move far on the railway at Peterborough without coming across a J6 0–6–0. Over one hundred were in service. Those at Peterborough were mainly used for light goods, brickyard shunting duties and engineering trains.

O4/7 No. 63634 stands in front of the old New England coaling plant. This engine was built by the Great Central in July 1912 and remained in service until September 1962, completing over fifty years service. The engine had recently been given a general overhaul when this photograph was taken.

This photograph of New England was taken while the depot was still open to steam, some four months before the last day of steam operation on 3 January 1965. The massive coaling tower stands behind the interesting steam travelling-crane used to empty the ashpits.

30.8.64

This rear view of No. 63634 shows the open cab fitted to these workhorses, which were for so many years a common sight on heavy mineral trains.

B1 No. 61138 stands at the south end of New England depot. Note the overhead watering system. Several B1s were allocated to New England.

30.8.64

In the last days of steam working at New England little variety remained. Here No. 43147 stands on shed. Note the tablet apparatus fitted.

30.8.64

O4/3 class No. 63833 was built for the ROD (Railway Operating Division) in the First World War, and later purchased by the LNER in 1925. The engine remained in service until January 1962.

In August 1964 time had run out for some 9Fs, including this one, No. 92176, which is pictured awaiting its final journey.

A number of run-down A3s remained at New England in the last days! No. 60065 *Knight of the Thistle* was one of them.

8.64

Standard 9F 2–10–0s were part of the New England scene right to the bitter end. No. 92164 was still active when this photograph was taken.

30.8.64

B1 No. 61109 stands next to an old tender used as a sludge carrier. In earlier days this spot would be packed with locomotives.

30.8.64

No. 64254, one of New England depot's many J6 0–6–0s, seen in the shed yard below the overhead water supply.

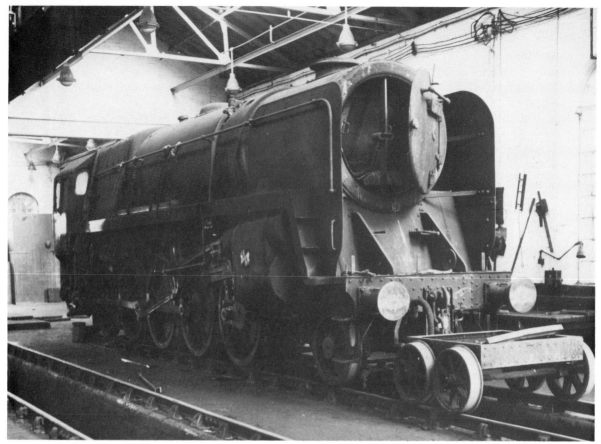

The valve gear has been dismantled on 9F 2–10–0 No. 92171. When this photograph was taken steam locomotives were still receiving alterations in the repair shops, though later very few would have been given attention.

30.8.64

The fitting of double chimneys considerably altered the appearance of the Gresley V2s. No. 60862 is here standing among several other redundant locomotives a month before its withdrawal and cutting up at Doncaster works.

23.6.63

A3 No. 60050 *Persimmon* awaits its fate at New England. The locomotive was in the final A3 form with double chimney and German-type smoke deflectors.

23.6.63

Class O4/8 No. 63606 of Frodingham depot receives attention in the repair shops at New England. This engine was built at Gorton works in 1913, being rebuilt to O4/8 in June 1955 and surviving in traffic for a further ten years.

30.8.64

4F 0–6–0 No. 43957 was a Peterborough Spital Bridge locomotive, seen here at the side of its home shed in March 1955. At one time a considerable number of 4Fs were allocated to the depot.

C12 No. 67368 photographed standing in the back of Peterborough Spital Bridge depot. The depot was a round-house design similar to many other Midland sheds.

When Spital Bridge depot became an Eastern Region shed several class J39 0–6–0s were transferred to the depot. No. 64951 stands at the side of the shed building.

No. 43066 stands outside the entrance to the round-house at Peterborough Spital Bridge. In front of the engine is a coke brazier; these were a familiar sight at depots to prevent the engines freezing up in severe weather.

Visiting 4F 0–6–0s were commonplace at Spital Bridge depot. No. 44182 was an 18D Staveley engine. Over seven hundred 4Fs were in service during the early fifties.

March Locomotive Depot

Five 'tram' locomotives from the Wisbech & Upwell Tramway stand disused on March shed, their duties having been taken over by diesels. The line up consists of four J70 0–6–0 tanks, and the only Y6 0–4–0T, No. 68083.

8.11.52

One of March depot's immaculate D16/3s, No. 62605. This engine was one of those members of the class which retained their original footplating. No. 62605, photographed at its home depot, was to remain in service for just over two more years.

13.3.55

O4/2 No. 63657 was one of the ROD locomotives introduced in 1917. These O4s had steam brake only and no water scoop.

13.3.55

WD No. 90064 in a reasonable external condition at March depot. The engine had probably received light repairs shortly before this picture was taken as the smokebox has been repainted.
23.3.63

Contrast in front end design of the LMR and ER class 5 mixed-traffic locomotives. An LMR class 5 and B1 No. 61003 *Gazelle* were caught by the camera during the last few months of steam working at March depot.

Several 'Britannias' were transferred to March depot when replaced by diesels. No. 70001 *Lord Hurcomb* is coaled and ready for its next duty.

9.9.62

'Britannia' class No. 70010 *Owen Glendower* at March. Several members of the class were to end up in store at the depot.

9.9.62

O1 No. 63746 at March, with the coaling-tower, known locally as 'The Wedge', in the background. The O1 remained in service until February 1964.

O1 No. 63687 had twelve months left in service when photographed, being withdrawn in October 1963 from March depot. After a period of storage it was moved to Doncaster works and cut up in February 1964.

J17 No. 65582 was probably in its last week of service when this photograph was taken, being withdrawn in September 1962.

J20 No. 64699 was the last of the twenty-five members of the class built and was also among the last withdrawn, the class becoming extinct in September 1962. No. 64699 was one of the class rebuilt with round-topped boiler.

O1 No. 63887 was still a March engine when this photograph was taken, in September 1962, being transferred to Staveley shed in the same month and remaining in traffic until February 1963, when it was withdrawn, and cut up at Doncaster works the following month.

9.9.62

B1 No. 61095 at March is here fitted with a self-weighing tender. In the back-ground is 4F 0–6–0 No. 43888. Several class 4Fs were at the depot at this time.

21.7.63

Visiting locomotives still worked in from distant depots during the last days of steam at March. WD No. 90722 was based in Yorkshire. In the last years of steam many of the WDs were to be seen in appalling condition.

In the last days of steam at March visitors from the London Midland Region were very common. In this photograph there are three; the engine nearest the camera is class 5 No. 45224.

21.7.63

The standard 4MTs were only introduced in 1953. Just nine years later No. 76034 is in store at March. Note the high running-plate on these engines.

This engine-only view of standard 4MT 76034 shows clearly the valve gears and connecting rods. Several members of this class have survived into preservation.

K3 No. 61880 stands at March after withdrawal, its tender having been emptied. K3s were inclined to rough riding, especially if due for a general overhaul.

9.9.62

Even LMR designs ended up stored at March. 4F No. 44509 still had a full tender of coal, although it is very unlikely that it worked again after this photograph was taken.

Many locomotives were in store at March when this photograph was taken, including several B1s, among them No. 61323. Note that the tender is still full of coal, though the chimney has received the customary piece of tarpaulin sheet.

9.63

Cambridge Locomotive Depot

Time was running out for B17/1 No. 61624 *Lumley Castle* when photographed in June 1952, as the engine was withdrawn in March of the following year, making it one of the first 'Sandringhams' to be withdrawn.

28.6.52

J17 No. 65502 stands ready to leave Cambridge shed. This engine was built at Stratford in 1900 and survived until September 1959. Cambridge depot had an allocation of nineteen J17s in the mid-fifties.

28.6.55

An interesting line-up at Cambridge depot. No. 68383 was a J66 0–6–0T, the class having been introduced in 1886. No. 42659, a Stanier 2–6–4T had worked in from Bletchley.

28.6.52

K2 No. 61780 stands at Cambridge in a very run-down condition. Note the smokebox door! The engine was fitted with a Westinghouse pump which was removed a few years later.
14.11.51

One of the graceful F6 2–4–2 tanks, No. 67227, at Cambridge. In spite of a period of storage at Cambridge this engine remained in traffic until 1958, when it was withdrawn from Colchester depot.
14.4.52

Only seven of the J66 class 0–6–0 tanks were in service in the fifties, several of these being in service stock. No. 68383 was a Cambridge engine which often performed shed-pilot duties.

Fairburn 2–6–4 tank No. 42155 and J15 No. 65390 stand over the ashpits at Cambridge. The LMR tank is lettered 'British Railways'.

17.5.52

Cambridge depot had a small repair shop. 'Sandringham' No. 61655 *Middlesborough* is receiving attention. Note the old coach body in the background.

17.5.52

Cambridge depot had several B2 class locomotives. These were rebuilds of B17s with two cylinders and 100A type boilers. No. 61617 *Ford Castle* was one; others included No. 61671 *Royal Sovereign*, which, unlike *Ford Castle* with its NE tender, had a standard LNER tender. This photograph was taken a year before the locomotive was withdrawn.

23.6.57

C12 No. 67397 had recently been transferred south from Hull Botanic Gardens depot when photographed at Cambridge in company with an E4, F6 and J68.

During the fifties several Great Northern C12 4–4–2 tanks spent a period of time at Cambridge.
Some, such as Nos. 67385 and 67367, were stored for a lengthy period.

Stored Great Eastern veterans at Cambridge included the E4 locomotive No. 62786 which is
unlikely to have worked again as it was withdrawn three months later, in July 1956.

3.4.56

Two veterans on 'The Dump': E4 No. 62784, and a Great Northern C12 4–4–2 tank No. 67360. An LNWR 0–8–0 was also in the line at this time, having worked from Bletchley and failed.

28.6.52

J17 No. 65585 is still to receive a front number-plate, the number having been painted on the buffer beam, as was LNER practice. No. 65585 was among the first members of the class to be withdrawn, which came just three years later.

14.11.51

D16/3 No. 62589 was one of the class rebuilt with a round-topped boiler, but it retained the original footplating and slide valves, whereas most of the class also received modified footplating.

3.4.55

E4 No. 62781 was restored to traffic after being stored for several months, during which time this photograph was taken. The engine was eventually withdrawn in January 1956. This E4 was built in 1892 and had worked in the north of England, being fitted with a side-window cab to give greater protection to the crew when working over Stainmore.

19.3.55

One of March shed's fleet of D16/3 locomotives, No. 62529, leaving Cambridge depot. Whenever one visited Cambridge at this time several 'Clauds' would invariably be in and around the shed and station.

10.4.53